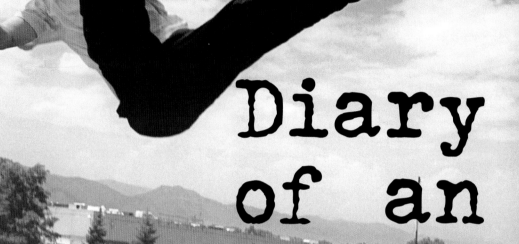

Diary of an INLINE SKATING Freak

Heinemann
LIBRARY

www.heinemann.co.uk/library
Visit our website to find out more information about **Heinemann Library** books.

To order:
 Phone 44 (0) 1865 888066

Send a fax to 44 (0) 1865 314091

Visit the Heinemann Bookshop at www.heinemann.co.uk/library to browse our catalogue and order online.

Produced by Monkey Puzzle Media Ltd
Gissing's Farm, Fressingfield, Suffolk IP21 5SH, UK

First published in Great Britain by Heinemann Library, Halley Court, Jordan Hill, Oxford OX2 8EJ, part of Harcourt Education. Heinemann is a registered trademark of Harcourt Education Ltd.

Author: Paul Mason
Editorial: Otto De'ath
Series Designer: Mayer Media Ltd
Book Designer: Mayer Media Ltd
Illustrator: Sam Lloyd
Production: Séverine Ribierre

Originated by Repro Multi-Warna
Printed in China by WKT Company Limited

ISBN 0 431 17541 1
08 07 06 05 04
10 9 8 7 6 5 4 3 2 1

British Library Cataloguing in Publication Data
Mason, Paul
Diary of an Inline Skating Freak
796.2'1
A full catalogue record for this book is available from the British Library.

Acknowledgements
With thanks to **Buzz Pictures** for supplying all photographs.

Every effort has been made to contact copyright holders of any material reproduced in this book. Any omissions will be rectified in subsequent printings if notice is given to the publishers.

Attention!

This book is about inline skating, which is a dangerous sport. This book is not an instruction manual or a substitute for proper lessons. Readers are advised to get lessons from a qualified instructor, always wear the right safety equipment, and never skate alone.

CONTENTS

Inline skating words are explained on page 30.

I AM AN INLINE SKATING FREAK

Brenden Connolly Fact File
Age: Sixteen
Occupation: Inline skater and school student
Likes: Buffy, Eminem
Dislikes: Sabrina, Dre
Music: Hip hop, rap
Hobbies: Skating, mixing

I am the mighty Brenden Connolly, the greatest inline skater that ever lived! Well, not yet I'm not, but one day I might be. There definitely can't be many skaters who are more into the sport than me. Ramps, skateparks, street obstacles, even skate hockey – I've tried them all. There can't be a kind of skating I haven't had a go at.

Brendan is not the greatest skater ever as he claims (I am!), but he's pretty good. We've been skating together for a couple of years now, and he's been keeping a diary with photos, stories, things we've cut out of magazines ... and this is part of it!

Errol

Me dropping in, making Errol wait for his go!

One day huge, adoring crowds will watch me doing massive jumps like this. Maybe...

DECEMBER

1	8	15	22	29
2	9	16	23	30
3	10	17	24	31
4	11	18	25	
5	12	19	26	
6	13	20	27	
7	14	21	28	

IN THE BEGINNING

Had my first go at inlining today. Errol took me down to a local park and lent me a pair of his old skates. It's a lot harder than it looks, and I was really glad he'd also lent me some pads. I just wish he'd lent me some padding for my bum, too!

I barely managed to skate along, although once I remembered how I used to ice skate it began to go a bit better. But Errol's really good: he was jumping about like a flea, sliding along a rail and doing spins in the air.

Errol doing a grind.

He wasn't always this good. His mum kept these photos of his wobbly first attempts at blading!

6

You need to build up to tricks like this slowly, starting with much smaller jumps. No one starts this big!

INLINE INFO

A few new words I've already come across:

'Hard' and 'soft' boots – 'hard boots' are like ski boots; 'soft boots' are more like trainers. Most people wear hard boots at first.

Chassis – the frame that holds the wheels.

Bearings – tiny metal balls inside the wheel that allow it to turn.

7

FEBRUARY

2	9	16	23
3	10	17	24
4	11	18	(25)
5	12	19	26
6	13	20	27
7	14	21	28
1	8	15	22	29

Bet this bloke wished he'd worn his pads...

NEW BOOTS

I'm really looking forward to getting my own skates and pads. The ghost of Errol's stinky feet is starting to haunt my bedroom at night! Looking around at the range of kit on offer is a bit scary – I know I won't be able to get another pair for a while, so the skates need to be the right ones for me.

Pads and helmet can look bulky, but I'm quite often glad of them!

Manager

	Time	Trans
✓ ...plete	< 1 minute	1 MB

Four styles of inline skating
Aggressive – sometimes called 'street': performing tricks and jumps in skateparks and on the street.
Hockey – like ice hockey, but on concrete.
Recreational – for fitness and pleasure.
Speed – going as fast as you can downhill.

8

Speed skaters use a lightweight rigid chassis and fifth wheel for greater speed.

LOW, FLEXIBLE CUFF HELPS WITH ADVANCED GRIND TRICKS.

LACE CLOSURE ALLOWS MORE FLEXIBILITY.

THICK INTERNAL PADDING ABSORBS SHOCKS.

SMALL WHEELS LEAVE LARGER GAPS FOR GRIND TRICKS.

CHASSIS WEAR PREVENTED BY GRIND PLATES AND BLOCKS BETWEEN WHEELS.

CHASSIS CLIPS AND AXLE BOLTS PROTECTED FROM BREAKAGE BY DEFLECTORS.

In the end I went for aggressive skates like these, because we like riding the skatepark so much.

OTHER SKATE TYPES:

Recreational – Main differences from aggressive skate: higher cuff for support, clip closure, bigger wheels for more speed, brake on left-hand boot heel (can usually be removed).

Hockey – Low cuff is flexible, soft wheels give good grip, less padding for more control.

APRIL

```
    5   12  19  26
    6   13  20  27
    7   14  21  28
1   8   15  22  29
2   9   16  23  30
3   10  17  (24)
4   11  18  25
```

GETTING GOING

The end of my first proper weekend riding with my new kit. I feel like I've really made progress: I can skate along fine, change direction and stop (but not very well!). Stopping's the hardest part: because I wanted aggressive skates, I've had to learn to stop without a heel brake on my boots. We took photos of someone using a heelbrake, and it looked a lot easier than T-stops and power slides, which are what I need to learn...

Just like with ice skating, you pick up speed by pushing off from your back foot, which is planted at an angle to your front foot.

Note to self:
Memorize where there are handrails you can grab hold of to stop!

1) THIS POWER-SLIDE BRAKING TECHNIQUE IS TRICKY TO LEARN. YOU SKATE BACKWARDS, AND USE YOUR BACK FOOT TO SLOW DOWN.

2) KEEPING YOUR KNEES BENT HELPS YOU TO ABSORB SUDDEN SHOCKS, AS WELL AS TO CONTROL THE SPEED OF YOUR BRAKING.

3) CLOSE UP YOU CAN SEE THE ANGLE OF THE SKATER'S BRAKE FOOT.

MAKING TURNS:

Changing direction is instinctive. Your body pretty much follows where you're looking. It helps to put the arm that's on the side you want to turn out in front of your body, but most people do this naturally. The key is to relax.

JULY

	5	12	19	26
	6	13	20	27
	7	14	21	28
1	8	15	22	29
2	9	16	23	30
3	10	17	24	31
4	11	18	25	

EMAIL FROM THE US

| Compose | Addresses | Folders | Options | Print | Help |
| Reply All | Forward | Delete | Previous | Next | Close |

To: Sarah Jane Meadowes
From: Brenden Connolly
Subject: Inline in the Big Apple
Date: Saturday, 10th July

Hi Sarah Jane! Mum tells me you're really into blading, but for fitness instead of tricks. I've just got into it too, but for tricks instead of fitness! So, what can you tell me about blading in New York?

To: Brenden Connolly
From: Sarah Jane Meadowes
Subject: Re: Inline in the Big Apple
Date: Wednesday, 14th July

My brother snapped this one as I was on my way out the other day! It's the only recent pic I've got, though.

Hey, Brenden! Yes, I go blading most weekends, usually in Central Park where there's a special track. Lots of people skate on the street, and there are even skate couriers: it's a neat way to get round the city. There are a few guys here who are into more tricksy skating: I've sent a couple of photos as proof. Fabiola da Silva is a really good female rider, and always does well in the X-Games.

FABIOLA DA SILVA
Nickname: Fabby
Born: Sao Paulo, Brazil
Birthdate: 18 June 1979
Height: 5 ft 2 in
Weight: 112 lbs.
Occupation: Pro skater
Competing since: 1995
Fabiola's the world's most influential female skater. In 2002 she revolutionized inline skating by starting to compete (and place highly) in men's vert contests.

Even if Sarah Jane just skates for fitness, there's obviously a thriving street scene in New York!

SEPTEMBER

	6	13	20	27
	7	14	21	28
1	8	15	22	29
2	9	16	23	30
③	10	17	24	
4	11	18	25	
5	12	19	26	

These guys just use a barrel on its side as the goal. There's plenty of friendly sitting around chatting in street hockey!

STREET HOCKEY

A friend of Sarah Jane's in America plays skate hockey, and she sent me some photos. I'd really like to have a go at it. I thought you must have to be a really good skater - but Sarah Jane says however good you are it's still loads of fun.

The equipment for serious inline hockey matches is different from normal skating gear, though for street hockey all you need is sticks. Most teams have a good kit-bag full of spares, though, so you can normally borrow gear for your first few goes.

Apparently there's a regular game on Sundays at one of the local parks. I think I might try to get along there!

Once the action gets going, everyone warms up quickly.

SKATE HOCKEY RULES

THESE ARE RULES FOR CLUB HOCKEY, BUT PEOPLE PLAY MORE INFORMAL GAMES WITH THEIR MATES:

● NO CHARGING, TRIPPING OR ROUGHING, OR HOLDING ON TO OTHER PLAYERS.

● NO AGGRESSIVE USE OF THE STICK.

● NO INTERFERING WITH A PLAYER WHO DOESN'T HAVE THE PUCK.

● PLAYERS MUST WEAR PROTECTIVE GEAR: HELMET; ELBOW, KNEE AND SHIN PADS, AND A GUMSHIELD.

The hardest thing is controlling the ball while skating fast.

OCTOBER

	4	11	18	25
	5	12	19	26
	6	13	20	27
	7	14	21	28
1	8	15	22	29
2	9	16	23	30
3	(10)	17	24	31

SKATEPARK

Our trip to the skatepark this afternoon was excellent fun. We spent most of our time on the mini-ramp, which is like a miniature half-pipe. The sides are nothing like as steep, and the transition from side to side looks longer. But you still seem to build up a lot of speed! It took me a while to get used to it, but Errol was already really good. He gave me a few pointers and by the end of the session I was dropping in OK. I even managed a couple of backside stalls on the opposite ramp.

LEARNING A NEW TRICK?

DO:

• Wear protective gear.

• Start small, then build up to bigger versions.

• Break the trick down into its component parts.

DON'T:

• Try a new trick before you feel ready because your mates say you should.

• Try a trick until you've watched other people do it several times.

I started on a small ramp with a wall beside it, which felt much safer!

1 WITH YOUR KNEES BENT, LEAN FORWARDS UNTIL YOU START TO ROLL DOWN THE RAMP.

2 KEEPING KNEES BENT TO ABSORB THE TRANSITION, ALLOW ONE FOOT TO ROLL AHEAD OF THE OTHER.

3 LEAN INTO THE UP-SIDE OF THE RAMP, KEEPING ONE FOOT FORWARD.

4 USE YOUR FORWARD FOOT TO BALANCE THE GRIND PLATE ON THE EDGE OF THE RAMP. STEP ON TO THE PLATFORM; WAVE TO THE ADORING CROWDS.

17

NOVEMBER

1	8	15	22	29
2	9	16	23	30
3	10	17	24	
4	11	18	25	
5	12	19	26	
6	13	20	27	
7	14	21	28	

1. I HAVE MY FRONT FOOT POINTING TWISTED OFF THE RAIL ON THE GRIND PLATE.

2. AS I STEP OFF, YOU CAN SEE THAT MY BACK FOOT HAS BEEN GRINDING ALONG PARALLEL TO THE RAIL.

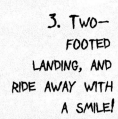

3. TWO-FOOTED LANDING, AND RIDE AWAY WITH A SMILE!

DAILY GRIND

After our last trip to the skatepark, Errol and I decided that next time we were really going to concentrate on learning some new tricks. We planned to spend a whole weekend at the park (making the most of the entry fee!). We made up a checklist of what to take, told our parents what we were planning to do, and we were off! My dad said I had to phone him at lunchtimes, 'Just so we know you're both OK.'

So many obstacles! Didn't have the courage for the moguls section this time. Maybe next trip?

18

I guess we've got a lot to learn still!

Hey, dough-boy, don't forget your food!
Errol

BRENDEN AND ERROL'S BIG DAY OUT

Stuff to take:

- All gear — skates, pads, helmet etc.
- Warm jacket for if it's chilly between sessions.
- Shorts, in case it's hot!
- Money and mobile phone for emergencies.
- Food — sandwiches, snacks, fruit — and water. Need to drink plenty, because we'll be working really hard!
- Backpack to take it all in!

19

NOVEMBER

1	8	15	22	29
2	9	16	23	30
3	10	17	24	
4	11	18	25	
5	12	19	26	
6	13	20	27	
7	14	21	28	

180 AIR

What a weekend! I can't walk another step, let alone skate anywhere. I woke up this morning after Day One feeling like my arms and legs had lead weights on them. I can't imagine what they're going to feel like tomorrow...

Still, it was a really good way of learning new tricks fast. On Saturday we worked on grinds: I just stuck with the soul grind, because it's the basis of so many other grinds and a really good one for beginners to learn. Today we worked on our ramp skills, especially the 180 air. One of the other skaters told me this is a great one for the skatepark, because it helps you to build speed on the ramps.

1) AS I HEAD FOR THE TOP OF THE RAMP I LET ONE FOOT LEAD THE OTHER, AND BEGIN TO TURN MY BODY.

2) MY LEAD LEG GOES INTO THE AIR, FOLLOWED BY THE BACK ONE. THEN I TURN MY HEAD AND BODY BACK TOWARDS THE RAMP.

3) LANDING ON THE DOWN SLOPE, KEEPING MY KNEES BENT TO ABSORB SHOCK AN GIVE BETTER BALANCE.

'Start small, grow big': lots of aerials rely on the speed and basic technique of the 180 air. And I can do one now!

APRIL

	4	11	18	25
	5	12	19	26
	6	13	20	27
	7	14	21	28
1	8	15	22	29
2	9	16	23	30
3	10	17	24	

Even third place won me a prize – some new shoes.

COMPETITION

Just home from my first competition: I really enjoyed it. It wasn't like a football match or something like that, with loads of rules. Lots of people turned up on the day and took it in turns to skate on the ramp and grinds. The only scary thing was that the pipe was a half-pipe, which I haven't ridden much before! You go a lot faster, and it's really important to be confident enough with the speed.

I stuck to tricks I know really well – I had enough to worry about without trying anything new! Lots of the people there are better skaters than me, but they tried more difficult aerials and fell. I managed to scrape third place, which I'm really pleased with!

This guy won the comp. He was really confident on the ramp.

22

These ESPN competitions feature the world's best skaters. Might be a while before I'm ready for one of these!

APRIL

4	11	18	25
5	12	19	26
6	13	20	27
7	14	21	28
1	8	15	22	29
2	9	16	23	30
3	10	17	24

FIGHTING FIT

Day seven of my new fitness drive, and already I feel worse! I wish I'd asked Sarah Jane about it before I'd started. Her email's full of loads of really useful advice...

Running off-road is more interesting than pounding the streets!

To: Brenden Connolly
From: Sarah Jane Meadowes
Subject: Re: Fitness drive
Date: Tuesday, 19th April

Brenden, you should have asked me about this before! I use my skates to keep fit, remember? Sounds like you started off trying to do too much at the start.

There are a few things to consider when you're trying to get fitter:
1. Plan your training, and stick to the plan. It's really tempting to do more if you're feeling good, but it's not a great idea.
2. Make sure you build in 'rest' days. These don't have to be 'do nothing' days, just ones where you only do gentle exercise.
3. It's more interesting if you mix up different types of activity.
I've attached a suggested training régime you might like to start with. Hope it helps!

PS Make sure you always warm up and warm down!

Shoulder stretch

Thigh stretch

Lower back/thigh stretch

Hamstring stretch

The speed needed for a grind this long means you need loads of leg strength.

File			fer
✓ Blading info.sit	Complete	< 1 minute	MB

Planning a training programme
- Start by planning four 45-minute training sessions a week.
- Do not train flat-out at first – roughly 75% effort is best.
- Mix up running, swimming, biking (on-road or off) and skating.

MAY

2   9   16   23   30
3   10 17   24   31
4   11 18   25
5   12 19   26
6   13 20   27
7   14 21   28
1   8   15   22   29

Name: Albert Hooi

Lives: Dublin, Ireland

Discipline: Street and ramp

Description: Albert is known as one of the most naturally talented skaters around, famous for the effortless way he picks up new tricks.

HEROES AND HISTORY

I've been digging around trying to find out more about the history of skating. Apparently there have been designs for inline skates for nearly 200 years. The early ones probably didn't catch on because they had iron wheels!

The first modern skates were made by Scott and Brennan Olson, ice hockey players from Minneapolis, USA. Their idea soon caught on, and before long it wasn't just ice skaters, skiers and hockey players who were using the new invention to scoot around.

Now, inline skating is a sport in its own right. These are some of the biggest names in skating today:

Name: Charlie Ashby

Lives: Orange County, USA

Discipline: Street and ramp

Description: An amazingly stylish skater, Charlie is the insider's choice for one of the smoothest skaters around. Often the underdog favourite in competition.

Name: Josh Petty

Lives: San Diego, USA

Discipline: Street and ramp

Description: Known for his colourful personality and stylish skating, Josh helped shape modern skating styles.

Name: Richard Taylor

Lives: Barry Island, Wales

Discipline: Street and ramp

Description: Regarded by his friends as 'the ultimate skater' Richard is equally at home with street or ramp tricks. One of the fastest skaters around, everything seems to happen at high speed when he's performing.

TOP FEMALE AGGRESSIVE SKATERS

Angela Araujo, Brazil – Fabiola da Silva says, 'I come home and find (Angela) asleep with her skates on. I can't keep up with her.'

Ayumi Kawasaki, Japan – Tiny, at 5'1" and 103 lbs; manages to combine being a pro skater with being a student.

Fallon Heffernan, USA – Even smaller than Kawasaki at 4'11" and 90 lbs, the Floridian says, 'I always feel like I can be better at everything... I'm just very competitive by nature.'

OCTOBER

3	10	17	24	31
4	11	18	25	
5	12	19	26	
6	13	20	27	
7	14	21	28	
1 8	15	22	29	
2 9	16	23	30	

Location: Temecula, USA

Name: various spots

Type of skating: Street

A famous street-skating location in Temecula; this is Mike Leaf skating a handrail. Warm weather and smooth concrete make for inline heaven!

INLINE HOTSPOTS

Another research job! My teachers would be amazed if they knew I was doing this much studying. It helps that it's an interesting subject, of course...

I used the Internet, my ever-growing collection of magazines and spoke to some of the older skaters at my local skatepark. With their combined information I've made a world map showing some of the top skate spots, divided between skateparks and street locations.

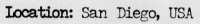

Location: San Diego, USA

Name: 'Mellow Yellow'

Type of skating: Street

This shot shows a famous handrail nicknamed 'Mellow Yellow'. There are loads of other spots in San Diego.

28

Location: Manchester, UK

Type of skating: Skatepark

The smooth concrete and huge bowls of Manchester's skatepark allow skaters, inline skaters and BMXers to build up speed for massive aerials.

Location: London, UK

Name: Playstation 2

Type of skating: Skatepark

The undercover ramps of Playstation 2 are popular with inline skaters, skateboarders and BMXers from all over London and the south-east of England.

Location: Marseille, France

Type of skating: Skatepark and street

Marseille's warm climate, palm-fringed skateparks and many street spots make it heaven for outdoor sports like inline skating and skateboarding.

INLINE SKATING WORDS

Aggressive skating
A style of skating that uses tricks including aerials and grinds.

Clip closure
A way of doing up boots tightly, excellent for sports such as inline skating. Clip closures are also used in ski boots and some types of motorcycling boots.

Cuff
The top part of an inline skating boot, where it ends and meets the back of the skater's calf.

Dropping in
Riding down the down-slope of a ramp at the start of a trick.

Flexibility
The ability to move easily. For example, someone who is able to bend over and touch their hands flat on the floor might be said to be very flexible. So might a piece of wood that can be bent without breaking.

Grinds
Tricks where the skater slides along a strip of concrete or metal, for example a handrail.

Half-pipe
A steep, large ramp that gets its name from looking like a section of giant pipe that has been cut in half.

Handrail
The rail, often made of metal, for people to hold on to while using stairs.

Mini-ramp
A smaller version of a half-pipe.

Power slide
A technique for braking inline skates.

Recreational
Recreational skating is done for fun and fitness, like jogging.

Speed skating
Inline skating where people try to reach the maximum possible speed.

Transitions
The gaps between actually skating. So, after going up a ramp, you have to turn somehow in order to go down it again. The turn is called a transition.

T-stop
A technique for braking inline skates.

Vert
Skating on a half-pipe ramp.

X-Games
An annual competition series made for TV. It has events around the world, showcasing inline skating, BMX, skateboarding, snowboarding and other extreme sports.

INTERNET LINKS

Most big skate companies have their own websites, which can be full of information about their riders, techniques, new products and links to other inline sites. Just key the company's name into a search engine to find them.

OTHER GOOD SITES INCLUDE:
www.iisa.org
Home site of the International Inline Skating Association, with information on equipment, places to skate, developing skills, and inline events and competitions.

www.inlineskating.about.com
General-purpose skate site that provides links to a variety of articles.

www.aggressive.com
An online resource for the aggressive skater community, with information on the pros, skate injuries and a 'help area' where you can get help learning tricks.

VIDEOS AND DVDS

Forest Fire and *Transcend* are both excellent videos put together by *Daily Bread* magazine.
his-to-ry is a DVD featuring skaters from the excellent Monx team.
Insiders is another DVD of aggressive skating, this time from members of the Kizer team.
Trash: United Front 2 showcases some of the best street skating ever seen on DVD.

BOOKS AND MAGAZINES

Activators: *Inline Skating* by Phil Perry
(Hodder Children's Books, 1999)

To The Limit: *Blading* by Martin Smith
(Wayland, 2000)

Unity
The leading UK-based inline mag, *Unity* focuses on aggressive street skating, featuring technique, equipment and locations around the world.

Daily Bread
A legendary American inline skating magazine.

Blue Torch
An online magazine for inline aggressive skaters.

DISCLAIMER
All the Internet addresses (URLs) Brenden has given in this book were valid at the time of going to press. However, due to the dynamic nature of the Internet, some addresses may have changed, or sites may have changed or ceased to exist since publication. While the author and Publisher regret any inconvenience this may cause readers, no responsibility for any such changes can be accepted by either the author or the Publisher.

31

INDEX

Titles in the *Diary of a Sports Freak* series include:

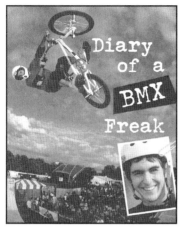

Hardback   0 431 17542 X

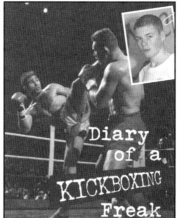

Hardback   0 431 17543 8

Hardback   0 431 17540 3

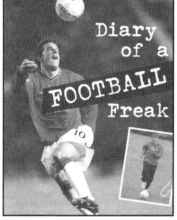

Hardback   0 431 17531 4

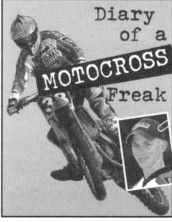

Hardback   0 431 17530 6

Hardback   0 431 17533 0

Hardback   0 431 17541 1

Hardback   0 431 17532 2

Find out about the other Heinemann Library titles on our website www.heinemann.co.uk/library